So You Call Yourself A Football Fan?

An Outhouse Trivia Book

By Christopher Forest

Dear readers,

Thanks so much for reading this edition of Outhouse Books. In *So you call yourself a football fan?* you will learn about the history, legends, and lore of everyone's favorite Sunday game. As you read, you can start by taking the quiz at the beginning and test your knowledge as you go. See if you are a Hall of Famer or a benchwarmer…or worse.

Hopefully you enjoy this brand of specialized reader. It is designed for those of you who like to have a sense of accomplishment, but have limited time to read. These quick readers can be completed in one session….even in the privacy of your own "outhouse."

We hope you enjoy! Happy reading!!!

Sincerely,
The Outhouse Staff

Outhouse Books

This book takes no responsibility for the claims made by way of the research conducted to complete it.

Outhouse Books also acknowledges all trademark rights to items mentioned in this text, including:
NFL™, Looney Tunes™, Wilson Footballs™, Cheeseheads™, and Campbell Soup™

Summary: A collection of interesting facts, trivia, and tidbits about American football.

Author: Christopher Forest
Editor: Melissa Forest

ISBN: 978-1481209212

Outhouse Books
Danvers, MA 01923
1 2 3 4 5 6 7 8 9 0 1

Take the quiz

Think you have what it takes to be a hall of famer? Here are the 100 questions that are answered in this book. Answer these questions first, then read the answers (yes, they are in order that the answers appear). Find out how football savvy you really are. Then, determine your score at the end. A longer space between questions denotes the answer is found in the following chapter.

What was the first game to resemble football?

What were the first footballs used in British style rugby?

How long was the earliest football field?

What was the first version of soccer to use hands (and eventually led to football)?

When did American football first begin in its earliest form?

What school invented the use of goal posts?

Where was the first football game played in America?

Why did colleges ban football in the 1860s?

When was the first official college football game played?

When was the first modern football game played between two teams?

Where did the first official rules for football come from?

During the late 1800s, how many players had been on each team, on the field, at one time?

Who created the "downs" system?

How many yards did it originally take to get a first down?

What was the Massasoit Convention?

Who was the first person to officially be paid to play in a game?

How did Theodore Roosevelt help form the NCAA and develop the forward pass?

Who was John Brallier?

When was the first professional football game played?

How much was a touchdown originally worth?

How much was a field goal originally worth?

Where was the first night football game player?

When was the first indoor football game held?

What was the World Series of Football?

What was the original name of the Chicago Bears?

How did the Cardinals get its name?

What football teams have shared their names with a baseball team from the same city?

Who were the Pirates?

What are the Packers named for?

What is the oldest team to still play football?

What team did the Raiders take the place of?

How much did the Giants cost when they joined the NFL?

On what date did the New Orleans Saints join the NFL?

A football was never really made with a pigskin, but why is it called a pigskin?

What shape were the first footballs?

What happened when the shape of footballs changed?

List three vital facts about footballs.

When were the numbers 00 and 0 banned in the National Football League?

When was the football helmet first worn?

Where did the term "touchdown" originate?

When did football helmets become popular to wear?

When did the football helmet become mandatory to wear?

Who coined the term "sack"?

What ancient civilization coined the word "hut"?

What is the official football of the National Football League?

How do you know your official NFL football is authentic?

What is used to weigh down most penalty flags?

During what football game was a scoreboard first used?

Where was the first college stadium built?

What was the first college team to wear team colors?

What team inspired a soup (or a soup can?)

What animal appeared on the cover of the 1993 University of Florida media guide?

What league was the forerunner to the National Football League?

How many teams were in the forerunner to the National Football League?

Who were the first champions of the APFA?

Who was the first president of the APFA?

What is the longest professional winning streak in American football?

When was the National Football League formed?

When did professional football do through what appeared to be a period of segregation?

Before 1932, how was the league champion determined?

What was the name of the original NFL championship trophy (when the league was called the APFA)?

What was the Thorp Cup?

What happened to the recordings of the first Super Bowl game?

What is the official score of a professional forfeit?

What is the only team to forfeit a game?

During the 1960s, how many stars were on the National Football League logo?

Which team has a logo on only one side of its helmet?

What was the first team to wear a logo on its helmet?

What fans came up with the nickname "Cheeseheads" for the Green Bay Packers fans?

Who were the only two players injured going out for a coin toss?

Which teams switched leagues when the AFL and NFL combined?

What team did William Shakespeare play for?

Which New York Yankee held a high school record for most touchdowns on kick and punt returns?

What teams played the first ever overtime game in NFL history?

Who was Burt Bell?

What player had his name misspelled on his jersey before starting a game at quarterback?

How long is half time?

How many footballs must a home team have ready to use at the start of an NFL football game?

What was the first Super Bowl to use Roman numerals?

What is the only NFL team to be retired?

Who chooses the team helmet or shirt to represent a player entering the NFL Hall of Fame?

Who presents a player to be voted on for enshrinement in the NFL Hall of Fame?

What was the first bowl game?

What was the first game to be televised?

Who first showed the best practical use of a forward pass?

Who was the grandfather of football coaching?

Who came up with the idea of putting numbers on football uniforms?

How did George Halas increase the popularity of football?

What changes occurred to the game in 1905?

Who was the first person ever drafted into the NFL?

When was a penalty flag first used in a professional game?

What network cover the first telecast of the NFL championship?

How much did it cost to purchase the rights to the first NFL championship?

Who was the shortest player to play in the NFL?

How many father and son pairs have played in the NFL?

What was the first NFL team to move to the west coast?

What is the NFL Triple Crown?

Who was the first African-American to play football?

Who was the oldest person to play in the NFL?

Who started the first Thanksgiving NFL game day tradition?

Early Football 101

What was the first game to resemble football?

Greek Football? The first version of football is believed to be a game called *Harpaston*. Mentioned in early literature, this Greek game involved players running on a field. Players earned points for their team by kicking a ball passed a goal line, running it past a goal line, or passing it to a player that had run past a goal line. There was no regulation on how long a field was and there were few rules. It appears that players could be stopped by ANY means necessary.

What were the first footballs used in British style rugby?

Bladder ball! In the 11th century, the first rugby style game surfaced in England. This game was a popular sport and included a unique ball – it was made out of a pig's bladder. Unfortunately, the game became so beloved that everyone wanted to play it and eventually people ended up dying as a result of collisions in the game. In time, the game was banned by the King of England.

How long was the earliest football field?

The longest yard! The original version of the English rugby game did have a wide field. Opponents would actually run the ball from their hometown into the middle of the opponent's hometown in an effort to score.

What was the first version of soccer to use hands (and eventually led to football)?

In the 1600s, people in Ireland began playing a version of soccer that included the use of fists to move the ball…one of the original precursors to football.

When did American football first begin in its earliest form?

Versions of American football began being played in the 1820s. Most of these early games involved two teams with a simple purpose – one team tried to run or kick a ball across the goal of another team.

What school invented the use of goal posts?

In the 1830s, the Rugby School of England had developed a game similar to the version of football we see today (ironically, many of the other schools were playing what is now considered soccer). The Rugby School's version of the game included 18-foot goal posts with crossbars and players running across a goal line. However, it varied greatly from modern football as well and, as you might imagine, became the rugby game beloved today.

Where was the first football game played in America?

The first football game in America was played on Boston Common in the 1860s. It was played by the Oneida Football Club, an organization formed by a local 16-year old student. Teenagers played on the first teams and many of the players became prominent citizens in Boston. Incidentally, the club still exists and has a president that pays a $50 fee to the city to keep the team intact.

Why did colleges ban football in the 1860s?

Death by Football. By the 1860s, the rough version of football was banned at many colleges. Most matches appeared more-like an excuse to participate in a rumble, and many players ended up hurt. In fact, the games sometimes ended in fatalities.

That's More Like It
Modern Football

When was the first official college football game played?

The first official college football game was held on November 6, 1869 between Rutgers and Princeton. The game was more a version of rugby than soccer with teams having 20 players on the field. Rutgers won the game 6 to 4 in front of about 100 spectators

When was the first modern football game played between two teams?

The first version of football resembling modern football was played in a match between McGill University from Montreal and Harvard College in 1876. While visiting Massachusetts, the Montreal team hoped to play a version of football that resembled rugby. Harvard wanted to play a more soccer-like game. The two schools compromised playing one game of each style.

Where did the first official rules for football come from?

In 1873, Columbia, Rutgers, Princeton, and Yale representatives met to form the IFA (or Intercollegiate Football Association). They came up with initial rules for the game that was beginning to resemble a sport more like American football. At the time, the teams agreed to have 15 players on the field.

During the late 1800s, how many players had been on each team, on the field, at one time?

During the late 1800s, Walter Camp, the football coach at Yale, can be credited with many of the modern traits of the game. He was no fan of the contemporary version of the game that was played at the time and had 15 players on the field per team. He suggested that the teams be limited to 11 players at a time.

Who created the "downs" system?

Down and out! Walter Camp also created the down system. Camp even standardized the length of the field to 100 yards.

How many yards did it originally take to get a first down?

First and five! Early versions of American football, under Walter Camp's advice, had players advance five yards for a first down. Teams had three chances (not four) to make a first down…when it was then still illegal to throw the ball. In 1906, he suggested creating a "ten yard for every first down" system to replace the five-yard for every first down system. In 1912, the game expanded and opened up when a fourth down as added.

What was the Massasoit Convention?

On November 23, 1876, the first rules for American football were made making the sport resemble the modern one. The event was held at the Massasoit House in Massachusetts and called the Massasoit Convention. Representatives from Columbia, Harvard, Princeton, and Yale came up with this initial set of rules.

Who was the first person to officially be paid to play in a game?

The William Heffelfinger was the first person to be paid to play for a football team. The Allegheny Athletic Association (AAA) paid him $500 to play against Pittsburgh Athletic Club on November 12, 1892. A Yale grad, Heffelfinger scored on a fumble and helped the AAA win 4-0. The AAA team actually made $621 that day, after paying Heffelfigner. However, Heffelfinger's claim to fame went unnoticed at the time. It took nearly 80 years for this information to become public.

How did Theodore Roosevelt help form the NCAA and develop the forward pass?

In 1905, colleges decided to hold a meeting to make improvements to the game at the request of President Theodore Roosevelt. A year later, the meeting was held. The forward pass was developed out of this meeting. The group that formed this meeting later became the National Collegiate Athletic Association, better known as the NCAA.

Who was John Brallier?

John Brallier became the first officially recognized football player to be paid
in his day. He appeared in a game on September 3, 1895, after signing a $10 contract to play for the Latrobe Athletic Club against the Jeannette Athletic Club. He was the first known player to play for pay (several other players had secretly done it, including William Heffelfinger). He is now actually probably the seventh player to actually play for money.

When was the first professional football game played?

In fact, the first professional game was placed between Latrobe YMCA and the Jeanette Athletic Club in 1895.

How much was a touchdown originally worth?

When is a touchdown not worth six points? Prior to 1898, a touchdown was worth 4 points. However, after 1898, the scoring rule was changed and it was worth 5 points.

How much was a field goal originally worth?

Converting a four pointer. Prior to 1909, a field goal was worth four points. But, in 1909 it got changed to three points.

Where was the first night football game player?

Friday night lights! The first night football game ever played was held in Elmira New York on November 21, 1902. The Philadelphia Athletics defeated the club known as Kanaweola AC by a score of 39 to 0. Ironically, the day was…a Friday.

When was the first indoor football game held?

More than a month after the first night game, on December 28, 1902, the first indoor game was held. This game featured the Syracuse A.C. playing against the New York team. Syracuse beat New York 5-0 in – you guessed it – Madison Square Garden.

What was the World Series of Football?

The first championship of organized football was called the World Series of Football. It was a five-team tournament held in 1902. The five teams to participate were called New York, the New York Knickerbockers, The Orange (New Jersey) AC, the Syracuse AC, and the Warlow AC. On December 28, 1902, Syracuse won the tournament by defeating New York. On that Syracuse team was a guard who would later become famous – Glen, (Pop) Warner. Incidentally, the initials AC mean Athletic Club

Team History

What was the original name of the Chicago Bears?

Dah Staleys! The Chicago Bears originally started out as the Decatur Staleys. They were started by the A.E. Staley company of Decatur in 1919 as a team representing the company. They moved to Chicago in 1921 and became the Chicago Staleys. They eventually settled on changing their name to the Chicago Bears in 1922.

How did the Cardinals get its name?

Birds on the brain. The Arizona Cardinals did not get their name from the red bird that is seen throughout the country. Instead, they got if from the color of their jerseys. The team, which was originally located in Chicago, purchased their jerseys from the University of Chicago. According to the Pro Football Hall of Fame, when someone suggested that the shirts looked a faded color red, their team owner, Chris O'Brien quickly responded, "they are cardinal red." And with that, a name was born!

What football teams have shared their names with a baseball team from the same city?

There have been some football teams that had the same names as Baseball teams. These include the St. Louis Cardinals, the Brooklyn Dodgers, The Pittsburgh Pirates, and the Cincinnati Reds.

Who were the Pirates?

Black and gold….argh! The Steelers were originally founded on July 8, 1933 as the Pittsburgh Pirates by Arthur Joseph Rooney. However, in 1940, the team decided to change their name. The team sponsored a contest where fans could offer suggestions for a suitable new name. The name Steelers was suggested by many fans as a testimony to the economic importance of steel to the city.

What are the Packers named for?

Get packing! In 1909, the Green Bay Packers were formed by Earl Lambeau and George Calhoun. The team received $500 for equipment from Lambeau's employer, the Indian Packing Company, as well as company field space for practices. The Packers won ten games and lost one that season. In 1921, the team was later awarded to John Clair who ran the Acme Packing Company (no relation to the fabled Looney Tunes company)

What is the oldest team to still play football?

That's an old team. The oldest team to still play football is the Morgan Athletic Club. Formed by a man named Chris O'Brien, the MAC played in Chicago's southside neighborhood. The team later was renamed the Normals, then was called the Racine (after a Chicago street) Cardinals. The were later renamed the Chicago Cardinals, then moved to St. Louis (as the Cardinals), then Phoenix (as the Cardinals), becoming the current Arizona Cardinals in 1994.

What team did the Raiders take the place of in the AFL?

The Oakland Raiders were formed in January, 1960. It became the eighth member of the fledgling AFL that was formed the year prior. The Raiders actually took the place of the Minnesota Vikings, an original AFL team that left the AFL to join the NFL.

How much did the Giants cost when they joined the NFL?

The New York Giants joined the NFL in 1925. The cost to purchase the franchise - $500. The late Tim Mara paid that price and eventually helped create one of the permanent franchises in the league. In fact, three seasons after its inception – in 1925 – the Giants won their first championship.

On what date did the New Orleans Saints join the NFL?

Strange coincidence – maybe. The New Orleans team, known as the New Orleans Saints, formed on November 1, 1966. Ironically – or perhaps not so – November 1 is All Saints Day.

Football Lingo

A football was never really made with a pigskin, but why is it called a pigskin?

A football is called a pigskin because it was once made from the part of a pig. However, it was never really the skin that was used, but the bladders. Sounds gross, but the bladders of pigs – in fact of many animals – proved easy to sew and blow up with air. So, why the change? Over time, it was discovered that such pigskins could indeed cause a little bit of "turmoil" if improperly handled during a game, resulting in the warping of balls. Once the vulcanization process of making rubber came into production in 1844, the need for "bladder balls" got replaced by more rubber versions.

What shape were the first footballs?

A football was not always the spherical shape that it is today. In the earliest versions of the sport, the football was designed to be round. However both man-made versions and animal bladder versions had difficulty retaining air, flattening the ball slightly. Eventually, games were stopped in order for balls to be re-inflated. Over time, this proved boring and particularly meddlesome, so the spherical shape was eventually dropped.

What happened when the shape of footballs changed?

The current football shape appeared in the NFL in 1934. Prior to this, footballs resembled a rugby ball. Ironically, as a result of the change, the number of dropkicks (which are still legal) diminished. Jim Thorpe happened to make drop kicks popular prior to this.

List three vital facts about footballs.

- one cowhide makes ten balls

- a football is made of four pieces and one lace

- there are 16 lace holes keeping the laces together

When were the numbers 00 and 0 banned in the National Football League?

A big zero! Before 1973, the numbers 00 and 0 could be worn on an NFL jersey. After 1973, when NFL uniform rules became stricter, no new jerseys were distributed with those numbers. A player who had worn 0 was George Plimpton (in a brief stint with the Detroit Lions). Jim Otto of the Oakland Raiders and Ken Burroughs of the Houston Oilers both wore 00.

When was the football helmet first worn?

The football helmet debuted in the Army-Navy game in 1893. A navy player, Admiral Joseph Mason Reeves, was given a helmet designed by a shoemaker from Annapolis. Naval doctors had suggested that Reeves wear a helmet in football games, fearing that another blow to his head – he apparently had suffered from others – might do permanent damage.

Where did the term "touchdown" originate?

Touch down! The term touchdown may have originated with the Rugby School version of football. Players were trying to "touch down" a ball behind the opposition's goal line. By doing so, they also had the chance to kick an extra point, called a "try-at-goal."

When did football helmets become popular to wear?

Until the 1930s, it was not mandatory to wear a helmet when playing football. In fact, the early football helmets were more like aviator caps and proved cumbersome. Many people refused to wear them.

When did the football helmet become mandatory to wear?

The football helmet became mandatory to wear in 1939. Part of the reason that the helmets became popular is that the Riddell company began making plastic helmets starting in 1938.

Who coined the term "sack"?

A sack! Deacon Jones was one of the most famous and feared defensive lineman of all time. The Hall of Famer became famous for his ferocious tackles. However, he also has another – perhaps more lasting – claim to football fame. He invented the term "sack" to describe tackling a quarterback.

What ancient civilization coined the word "hut"?

Ever wonder why quarterbacks say the word "hut?" It is not a reminder of the cozy house they wish to retreat to during the off season in the Caymans. The command actually dates back to ancient Roman. Roman army leaders would use the word "hut" to signal that a command had to be followed (or, at the time, "executed"). March, "hut" mean the soldiers had to march. So, when a QB shouts hut, he is ordering an execution…of sorts.

What is the official football of the National Football League?

The official football of the NFL is the Wilson Football. They began supplying footballs to the NFL in 1941.

How do you know your official NFL football is authentic?

Authenticate it. Did you ever wonder if that game ball you received was really an official NFL game ball? Well, just look for the W. The Wilson company puts a "W" watermark on their footballs to ensure that they are authentic.

What is used to weigh down most penalty flags?

What weighs down those penalty flags – beans or sand. Incidentally, the flags were red in college until the 1970s and are orange in the Canadian Football League.

College Football 101

During what football game was a scoreboard first used?

Turkey scores! The first time a college scoreboard was used occurred on November 30, 1893. The scoreboard was invented by Arthur Irwin of Boston and used at the Thanksgiving Game between Harvard and Pennsylvania. At the end of the day, the scoreboard showed that Harvard beat Penn 18 - 8.

Where was the first college stadium built?

The first college stadium to house a football crowd was built by Harvard College in 1903. The first game played there was a bout between Harvard and Dartmouth on November 14, 1903. Harvard lost 11-0.

What was the first college team to wear team colors?

The first time a team wore colors appears to be June 8, 1875. On that day, the Harvard football team was outfitted in white uniforms with crimson trim and crimson stockings. They faced off against the team from Tufts.

What team inspired a soup (or a soup can)?

The team that inspired a soup. Cornell University is known for their football college colors of red and white. But, what many people do not know is that the Campbell Soup can colors were inspired by the Cornell colors. In 1898, Herberton Williams, an employee at Campbells, convinced the company to adopt the Cornell colors.

What animal appeared on the cover of the 1993 University of Florida media guide?

Ooops! In 1993, the University of Florida Gators made quite a gaffe on their media guide. Although they planned to put a beloved alligator on the cover, they accidentally placed a crocodile there.

NFL History 101

What league was the forerunner to the National Football League?

The first professional football teams were part of the American Professional Football Association founded in 1920. The founding organization – Hupmobile Dealership - was located in Canton, Ohio. There were 11 charter members of the league and two still remain. They are the Decatur Staleys (better known as the Chicago Bears) and the Chicago Cardinals (better known as the Arizona Cardinals).

How many teams were in the forerunner to the National Football League?

The earliest professional league was called the American Professional Football Association (more on them later) or the APFA. It consisted of 14 teams. Each team had to pay $100 to join the league.

Who were the first champions of the APFA?

The Akron Pros were the first champions of the American Professional Football Association. Of the eleven teams that played that year, only four teams actually finished the season.

Who was the first president of the APFA?

Jim Thorpe served as the first president of the American Professional Football Association. He also played for one of the teams, the Canton Bulldogs. The Canton Bulldogs fielded a team from 1920 to 1923 and 1925 to 1926. They won the championship in 1922 and 1923.

What is the longest professional winning streak in American football?

Streaking! The longest professional winning streak in American football also belongs to the Canton Bulldogs. During the 1921 to 1923 season, they won a record 25 games in a row.

When was the National Football League formed?

The National Football League was born in 1920 as the result of a merger between several smaller professional leagues. They formed the American Professional Football Conference at the Hupmobile automotive dealership in Canton Ohio. Two years later, it was reorganized and officially named the National Football League

When did professional football do through what appeared to be a period of segregation?

Between 1927 and 1946, the early NFL went through a period of what appeared to be segregation. African-American players were not signed for a some time. Prior to that time, only a handful of African-American players had played in the league- Fritz Pollard and Bobby Marshall were the first two African American players to join the NFL.

Before 1932, how was the league champion determined?

In 1932, a playoff game helped to determine who won the league championship. Prior to that, a team's won-loss percentage helped determine who was the league champion.

What was the name of the original NFL championship trophy (when the league was called the APFA)?

Where's the Lombardi Trophy? The Brunswicke-Balke Collendar Cup was the original name for the championship trophy awarded to the winner of the American Professional Football Association (the forerunner of the NFL). The cup was donated by the tire division of the Brunswicke-Balke Collendar company. The silver cup actually disappeared in 1920 – the year it was conceived – over disputed claims as to the winner that year. No one knows what happened to the cup to this day….or if they do, no one is talking.

What was the Thorp Cup?

The Thorp Cup? From 1934 until 1970, the championship trophy was known as the Ed Thorp Memorial Trophy. Thorp was a sporting goods dealer and noted referee who passed away in 1934. In 1970, the merger of the AFL and NFL created a new cup – the Vince Lombardi Trophy – now used today.

What happened to the recordings of the first Super Bowl game?

No known tapes of the first Super Bowl between the Green Bay Packers and Kansas City Chiefs still exist. The game itself was considered a foregone conclusion – most people believed that Green Bay would win. Ironically, it was played on both CBS (which held the rights for the NFL games) and NBC (which held the rights for the AFL Games). Incidentally, Green Bay won 35-10.

Did You Know???

What is the official score of a professional forfeit?

When a game is officially forfeited by one team, the final score is deemed 2-0. The reason to use a safety as a score is actually simple. A safety is the only score in football that is given to a team, not an individual.

What is the only team to forfeit a game?

We give up. The only forfeit in professional American football occurred on December 4, 1921, when the Rochester Jeffersons lost by forfeit to the Washington Pros/Senators. The league was new and the score at that time was officially posted as 1-0.

During the 1960s, how many stars were on the National Football League logo?

From 1960 to 1969, the NFL football logo was slightly different from the current logo. However, it had only 22 stars on the top part of the crest. And, the middle portion of the crest had ten black vertical stripes behind the words NFL.

Which team has a logo on only one side of its helmet?

One sided! Most teams have logos on their helmets – except, of course, the Cleveland Browns. But, can you name the team that has the logo on only one side of the helmet (most have it on two sides)? Well, the next time your watching a Steeler game, look closely. The logo is on only one side of the helmet.

What was the first team to wear a logo on its helmet?

NFL players began wearing logos on their helmet in 1948. The first team to wear them was the Los Angeles Rams. Fred Gehrke, a Rams player and freelance artist, hand-painted the well-known Rams logo on 70 helmets that year.

What fans came up with the nickname "Cheeseheads" for the Green Bay Packers fans?

Cheeseheads are the affectionate name that Green Bay Packers go by. However, initially the nickname was not so affectionate. It was believed to be developed by Chicago Bear Fans in 1987 as a way to poke fun of the rival fans from the dairy state. The Packer fans adopted the nickname and began using it to describe themselves. In fact, fans today even where foam cheeses on their heads at games. The nickname is also used between to describe Brewer fans. Incidentally, the word is trademarked by Foamation, Inc.

Who were the only two players injured going out for a coin toss?

Talk about strange injuries. In 1981, then Baltimore Colts were playing at the then St. Louis Rams. Colts offensive lineman Robert Pratt was running out for the coin toss when he suddenly came up injured. The reason – pulled hamstring when running from the sideline. A similar injury happened 40 years earlier, when Redskin captain Albert Edwards was returning from a coin toss against the Giants. Edwards had a history of knee problems and when he turned to go back to the sidelines, he heard a pop in his knee. The result was a career ending knee injury.

Which teams switched leagues when the AFL and NFL combined?

Switching Leagues. The Baltimore (and now Indianapolis) Colts, and Pittsburgh Steelers, were not always in the AFC. Prior to the merger of the AFL and NFL, the Colts were originally part of the NFL. Most NFL teams joined the NFC, except for the Colts and Steelers.

What team did William Shakespeare play for?

In 1936, the Pittsburgh Steelers made football and literary history by drafting a unique halfback from Notre Dame. The player was not unique for his abilities, but rather for his name – William Shakespeare.

Which New York Yankee held a high school record for most touchdowns on kick and punt returns?

Roger Maris was a famous New York Yankee. But, he did hold a football record for some time. He was the single game record holder for most touchdowns scored on kick and punt returns as a high school player. In one game, he actually scored four touchdowns on returns.

What teams played the first ever overtime game in NFL history?

The Giants and Colts played the first ever overtime game in NFL history. And, was it a doozy! The two teams were playing for the NFL championship in 1958. The game went into overtime at 17 – 17. The Giants got the ball first in overtime, failed to convert, but the Colts struck next, winning the game 23 to 17.

Who was Burt Bell?

From 1949 to 1956, Burt Bell was the commissioner of the NFL. Some people believe he helped single-handled save the NFL from disintegrating due to competition from rival leagues.

What player had his name misspelled on his jersey before starting a game at quarterback?

Bill Kenney was drafted by the Kansas City chiefs in 1978 and later cut during training camp. He made the team as a backup quarterback in 1980. Later in the season, normal starting quarterback Steve Fuller was unable to play and Kenney had to take his place. However, as luck would have it, the team spelled his name wrong on that particular game day jersey. And that is how *Bill Kenny* became quarterback.

How long is half time?

Halftime, by NFL rules, is 12 minutes long. That is why you can't take too long getting your snacks together.

How many footballs must a home team have ready to use at the start of an NFL football game?

A home team must have 24 balls ready to be used during a football game prior to kickoff. The league then provides an extra 12 balls, used in kicking situations, to insure the integrity of the footballs.

What was the first Super Bowl to use Roman numerals?

Super Bowl 4? The first Super Bowl to have a Roman numeral was not the actual first Super Bowl. Super Bowl IV (four for those who don't know) was the first championship that had a Roman numeral.

What is the only NFL team to be retired?

Retiring a team! You've heard of retired players and retired numbers, but believe it or not, the NFL has a retired name as well. When the Houston Oilers moved to Tennessee and became the Tennessee Titans, the NFL stepped in to prevent the Oilers name from being used again. It is officially retired.

Who chooses the team helmet or shirt to represent a player entering the NFL Hall of Fame?

When a player is elected to the NFL Hall of Fame, and played for many teams, he does not need to worry about which helmet or shirt will be enshrined with him. All teams are treated equally when the player is enshrined (unlike major league baseball).

Who presents a player to be voted on for enshrinement in the NFL Hall of Fame?

Did you ever wonder who officially presents the name of a person to be nominated to the football Hall of Fame. None other than the official media members who vote on the hall of fame…better keep those media members on your good side.

Historic Moments

What was the first college bowl game?

The first bowl game was held in 1902 in Pasadena, California. That year, the Rose bowl feature a 4-0 shellacking of Stanford at the hands of Michigan. The game started a long-standing tradition of bowl games…and at the time, the Rose Bowl crowned the college football champion. So much for the BCS

What was the first football game to be televised?

Talk about hitting the waves. The first college game ever to be televised was between Fordham University and Waynesburg College. Aired in September 1939, Fordham won 34-7. This college game actually predates the first televised professional game by one month. In October, 1939, the Brooklyn Dodgers took on the Philadelphia Eagles in a football match. Brooklyn (not to be confused with their baseball team) won 23-14.

Who first showed the best practical use of a forward pass to win a game?

Although the development of the forward pass occurred in 1906, it took seven years for its use to become evident. In 1913, Notre Dame players Knute Rockne and Gus Dorias showed off the value of the pass in a game against West Point.

Who was the grandfather of football coaching?

The grandfather of football coaching is often deemed to be Amos Alonzo Stagg. He introduced many new concepts to the ranks of football, including huddles, the end around play, and punt formation. He was coach for 57 years at Springfield College. He developed the tackle dummy and trick plays as well. And, baseball fans can thank him, too. He came up with the idea of a batting cage.

Who came up with the idea of putting numbers on football uniforms?

Numbers up! Ever wonder who came up with the idea of putting numbers on football uniforms. You can thank Amos Alonzo Stagg. He started the trend

How did George Halas increase the popularity of football?

George Halas, coach of the Chicago Bears, can be credited with helping to raise the popularity of the game. In 1925, he led his team on an 8 game in 12-day barrage which is unparalleled to this day. This barnstorming tour help hook many fans in the early 1900s. And there was no bye week in between.

What changes occurred to the game in 1905?

In 1905, rule changes helped put an end to violence in football. In the early 1900s, at least 18 deaths and 159 major injuries were attributed to the game. Then President Theodore Roosevelt "led the charge" (as he as good at doing) to change the game. The rule changes eliminated a flying wedge, encouraged the use of safety equipment (such as helmets) and made it mandatory to have only seven men at the line of scrimmage. As you may know from an earlier question, the forward pass was also developed at the time.

Who was the first person ever drafted into the NFL?

The first person ever drafted in the NFL??? That distinction belongs to Jay Berwanger. On February 8, 1936, he was selected as the first player ever drafted by the Philadelphia Eagles. He had been the Heisman Trophy Winner at the University of Chicago the year before.

When was a penalty flag first used in a professional game?

The penalty is on us. The NFL first used a penalty flag on September 17, 1948. It debuted in a game between the Green Bay Packers and the Boston Yanks. The flags must have been used a lot that evening…there were 12 penalties called on Green Bay and ten on Boston. Incidentally, Green Bay won 31 to 0. The flag came to the NFL from the college game (where it debuted in 1941). The flag was originally yellow, then turned white, and in 1965 turned yellow again.

What network cover the first telecast of the NFL championship?

The first televised telecast of the NFL championship game occurred in 1951. The game was held on December 23 of that year. Do you know which network broadcast that original game… chances are you don't. It was aired on the defunct Dumont Network, which operated from 1946 to 1956. The Los Angles Rams (formerly of Cleveland) beat the Cleveland Browns 27-14.

How much did it cost to purchase the rights to the first NFL championship?

Big bucks! The Dumont Network paid at least $75,000 to purchase the rights to air the game (a few sources put it at $95,000, but most suggest $75,000).

Who was the shortest player to play in the NFL?

The shortest NFL player in the NFL history was Jack Shaprio. Nicknamed Soapy, this squeaky clean player was 5'1" and weighed 119 pounds when he played for the Staten Island Stapletons in 1929.

How many father and son pairs have played in the NFL?

Like father, like son. According to the NFL Pro Football Hall of Fame, there have been at least 197 fathers and sons who have played professional football.

What was the first NFL team to move to the west coast?

The first major professional sports team on the west coast was the Los Angeles Rams. They moved from Cleveland to L.A. in 1945.

What is the NFL Triple Crown?

The Triple Crown? Yes, the NFL does have one. The triple crown is given to the player who leads the NFL in three major categories from the three sides of the ball (defense, offense, and special teams). And yes, someone has won the award. The first winner was Sammy Baugh of the Washington Redskins. He won the Triple Crown while playing for the Washington Redskins in 1943. He led the NFL is passing, interceptions, and punting that season.

Who was the first African-American to play football?

Charles Follis became the first African American to play professional football. He was a halfback who signed to play with the Shelby Athletic Club in 1904, a team in the Ohio League.

Who was the oldest person to play in the NFL?

Age doesn't matter. The oldest person to play in the NFL was George Blanda. The quarterback and kicker retired from the Oakland Raiders in 1975 at age 48.

Who started the first Thanksgiving NFL game day tradition?

The Thanksgiving Football tradition traces its origin back to 1934. In that year, radio owner G.A. Richards decided to host a game between the 10-1 Detroit Lions (the team he owned) and the 11-0 world champion Chicago Bears. The games was played at the Univesity of Detroit stadium in front of 26,000 fans. Chicago won 19-16, but in reality, fans won. The thanksgiving games have been played ever since (except for the war years of 1939-1944).

Resources

The following are the main resources used to gather and validate information for this book. Check them out for more interesting football facts!

"1951 NFL Standings" *Philadelphia Eagles. Net* URL: http://philadelphia-eagles.net/pre-history/1951-stats.html

"American Football: Little Known Facts." *Voices.Yahoo.com.* URL: http://voices.yahoo.com/american-football-little-known-facts-about-376537.html?cat=14

Bonander, Ross. "Five things you did not know about the NFL." URL: http://www.askmen.com/toys/special_feature_150/168b_special_feature.html

Brooks, Andrew. "Harvard Stadium". Harvard Gazette. URL http://www.hno.harvard.edu/gazette/2003/10.23/00-stadium.html

"Football Firsts." *Professional Football Hall of Fame.* URL: http://www.profootballhof.com/history/release.aspx?release_id=1476

"Football History." *Sports Knowhow.* URL http://www.sportsknowhow.com/football/history/football-history-2.shtml

"Football Urban Legends Revealed #14." *Legends Revealed.* URL: http://legendsrevealed.com/sports/2010/06/04/football-legends-revealed-14/

Harvard Football Timeline. *The Game*.Org. URL http://www.the-game.org/history-timeline-harvard.htm

History of Football. *Hornet Football.* URL: http://www.hornetfootball.org/documents/football-history.htm

History of the Football Helmet. *Pasttimes Sports.* URL: http://www.pasttimesports.biz/history.html

"The History of the NFL." *MMBolding.Com.* URL: http://www.mmbolding.com/BSR/CFL_NFL_NFL_History.htm

"History and Origin of the Pittsburgh Steelers Logo." http://pittsburgh.about.com/od/steelers/a/logo.htm

"How Well Do You Know The Game?" URL: http://www.wilson.com/en-us/football/nfl/wilson-and-the-nfl/trivia/

Logos. *Chris Creamer's Sports Logos.net.* URL http://www.sportslogos.net/league.php?id=7

NFL History by the decade – 1969 to 1910: *NFL.Com.* URL http://www.nfl.com/history/chronology/1869-1910

NFL 1958 championship game films. *Rare Sports Films.* URL: http://74.125.47.132/search?q=cache:YvOJvrhHXDwJ:www.raresportsfilms.com/1958nflchampgame.html+giants+%2B+colt+%2B+first+overtime+game&cd=1&hl=en&ct=clnk&gl=us&client=firefox-a

"Penalty Flag." *Sporting Charts.Com.* URL: http://www.sportingcharts.com/dictionary/nfl/penalty-flag.aspx

Pro football history: *Pro Football Hall of Fame.* URL: http://www.profootballhof.com/history/general/birth.jsp

Penn Football in the 1800s: *Varsity Team History.* URL: http://www.archives.upenn.edu/histy/features/sports/football/1800s/origins.htm

How did you do?

100 questions correct – You're a Hall of Famer.

90 – 99 questions correct – Hoist that Lombardi trophy.

80-89 questions correct – You're the championship MVP.

70-79 questions correct – You're worthy of the game ball.

60-69 questions correct – Your almost ready for prime time.

50-59 questions correct – You can play in sub packages.

40- 49 – You've been signed to the practice squad.

30-39 – You're going through waivers.

20 -29 questions correct – You've just been cut for the third time.

10-19 questions correct – Hmmm, you might be Mr. Irrelevant.

0-9 questions correct – Water boy (or girl)!

Thanks for reading! We hope you've learned a little more about one of America's favorite sports.

Please look for more Outhouse Books. In the meantime, enjoy your football games!

Made in the USA
Lexington, KY
13 December 2016